THINE IS THE KINGDOM

THINE IS THE KINGDOM

By

JAMES S. STEWART, D.D.

Professor of New Testament Language, Literature and Theology
in the University of Edinburgh
Chaplain to the Queen in Scotland

CHARLES SCRIBNER'S SONS, *New York*

LIBRARY OF CONGRESS CATALOG CARD NUMBER 56-12446

To

MY MISSIONARY FRIENDS

across the seas

'He calleth His own by name, and leadeth them
out; and they follow Him, for they know His voice'

PREFACE

THIS little book on the theme of missionary motivation is based on lectures recently delivered in Scotland and in the United States. It does not attempt anything so ambitious as to sketch a theology of missions. What I have tried to do is to outline one particular path towards such a theology and to indicate certain basic prolegomena for the quest. I am sure we need constantly to remind ourselves that the imperative of the Church's mission to the world to-day rests solidly upon the indicative of the mighty acts of the Incarnation, the Cross and the Resurrection, and that the dynamic for our unaccomplished task is the accomplished deed of God. This is what these pages endeavour to set forth.

JAMES S. STEWART

New College,
The University of Edinburgh

CONTENTS

THE BASIC MOTIVE

SOMEONE once asked Dr Samuel Johnson what was the best argument for prayer. 'Sir,' replied the Doctor, 'there is no argument for prayer.' He did not mean that prayer is sophistry and delusion. He meant that everything in life is the argument for it. So if anyone to-day should ask, What is the best argument for missions?—the answer quite briefly is, There is no argument for missions. The total action of God in history, the whole revelation of God in Christ—this is the argument.

It is well that from time to time we should clarify our minds at this point. What is the basic motive of the Church's missionary enterprise? Different generations have stressed different aspects of the matter.

Thus, for example, some have based everything on our Lord's *Commission*. Did not Jesus say explicitly, 'Go ye and teach all nations'? Here, then, is our missionary charter. Here is a chapter-and-verse directive that forecloses all discussion. Behind all the romance and heroism of the thin red line of missions down the centuries stands Matthew 28.19, 20. As long as that text rings out its trumpet-toned commission, any man who opposes missions is implicitly saying he knows better than Christ.

This is indeed a valid argument. Nevertheless, this isolating of a single text is not an adequate account of missionary motivation. Suppose the last sentences of Matthew had been lost (as may indeed have happened with the Gospel of Mark), suppose mutilation of the papyrus roll had deprived us of the great commission, would the missionary challenge have been in doubt? Surely not! For it is no single injunction that has given the Church its marching-orders. The imperative is there, staring at us on every page of the Gospels, implicit in every word Jesus ever spoke, sealed for ever by His death and resurrection: 'the expiation,' cries John, 'for our sins, and not for ours only but for the whole world!'

A second motive which often in the past produced missionary concern has been *Compassion*. Pity for the 'blind benighted heathen' has overflowed in sacrificial service. The hungry multitude must be fed with the bread of life. Frequently this compassion has had an eschatological colour. It has been reinforced by the doctrine of final judgment. Without Christ, the pagan world was lost eternally and every single soul destined to endure the torment of the damned. Rescue the perishing! For pity's sake, snatch lost souls out of a ruined world! This was the motive. And it will be an ill day indeed for the Church when this driving, passionate sense of urgency vanishes away.

Yet this is not enough. It is too negative and narrow a foundation to bear the weight of the great creative enterprise of faith. And of those who saw heathenism as a *massa perditionis* not all recognised the Spirit of God brooding over the chaos and even in strange cults and alien creeds preparing the way for Christ.

If Commission and Compassion have been two motivating keynotes, a third is *Community*. To-day as never before we are realising our common brotherhood in the human family and our corporate responsibility. Is there any point to-day at which we can draw the line and say 'Here our responsibility ends'? Even if Jesus had never challenged us to a world view, life itself—by interlocking us inextricably together—would force that view upon us. To talk of being 'members one of another' is not just religious phraseology: it is desperate economic fact. How, then, is true community to be achieved? We Christians believe that in the Body of Christ we have the answer. Must we not therefore seek to extend this fellowship until it is coterminous with humanity? In days like these, can any Church be other than a pathetic pietistic backwater if it is not first and fundamentally and all the time a world missionary Church? Amid all competing nationalisms, Christianity emerges as the one true internationalism; above all outbursts of racialism, it stands as the final universalism.

Here is a mighty missionary motive—Community. Yet, strongly as it operates to-day, it is not enough. That man may be reconciled to man, nation to nation, is a noble vision indeed. But this is not in itself the startling, overwhelming good news that shattered history at the Cross and the Resurrection and launched Christianity like a thunderbolt upon the world.

A fourth notable missionary motive may be summed up in the word *Continuity*. Always the Church has felt constrained to continue the work which Jesus and the apostles began. That Jesus carried the mission of the Kingdom upon His heart, that it was His deliberate intention to call into being a Messianic society in which that mission would be exercised continuously to the end of time, that the Church of the New Testament was passionately missionary minded —all this admits no doubt whatever: and this, therefore, is the pattern to which Christendom must ever conform. We ourselves are the product of a mission: if the Church of earlier days had not sent out a Ninian, a Kentigern, a Columba, an Augustine, where should we have been? It was a foreign mission which built every Church in our land to-day. And the great new fact of our era, the ecumenical Church, would never have emerged into history but for the missionary labours of generations past. Thus it is our bounden duty to remember the rock whence we were hewn, to follow the example laid down in the Gospels and the Acts, and to continue the crusade that runs right back across the centuries to its origin in the mind and intention of Jesus.

Yet this motive, like the others, has its limits; and it may be doubted whether even the most vivid sense of historical obligation and ecclesiastical continuity holds dynamic enough to galvanise the soul of Christendom into fresh activity and set the Church on fire with evangelising zeal and passion.

There, then, are four words—Commission, Compassion, Community, Continuity—each of them representing at some period of the Church's life a major element in missionary endeavour. But none of these, nor all of them taken together, can constitute the basic argument. None of them touches the true profundity of this matter. In the last resort, the one reason for missions is *Christ*. He only is the motive, God's presence in Him the one sufficient cause.

The fact is, belief in missions and belief in Christ stand and fall together. To say 'I believe that God so loved the world that in Christ He gave everything He had, gave His very self', to use such words not lightly or conventionally but in spirit and in truth, means that the one who uses them binds himself irrevocably to make self-giving the controlling principle of life: and this is the very essence of mission. To put it otherwise, the concern for world evangelisation is not something tacked on to a man's personal Christianity, which he may take or leave as he chooses: it is rooted indefeasibly in the character of the God who has come to us in Jesus. Thus it can never be the province of a few enthusiasts, a sideline or speciality of those who happen to have a bent that way. It is the distinctive mark of being a Christian. To accept Christ is to enlist under a missionary banner. It is quite impossible to be (in the Pauline phrase) 'in Christ' and not participate in Christ's mission in the world. In fact, here is the surest test whether we have truly grasped what Christ was doing by His life and death and resurrection, or whether we have failed even to begin to understand the Gospel that He brought. James Denney once heard a distinguished missionary say—'Some people do not believe in missions. They have no right to believe in missions: they do not believe in Christ.' That stringent comment is a salutary reminder that a missionary outlook is a direct inevitable deduction from a saving knowledge of Jesus. The sole ground of missionary endeavour is Christ.

II

PERSONAL RELIGION AND WORLD CRUSADE

WE have seen the motive. Observe now that there are two elements which enter into it. One is the constraint of Christ upon the individual life. The other is the kingship of Christ over history. Each of these must be considered in turn.

On the one hand, the missionary urge is *the passion to share a personal discovery.* If we have ever been gripped by an over-powering sense of personal indebtedness to Christ; if we have really encountered the living Lord in the secret places of our own souls; if we have begun to see faith as Bishop Aulén defines it, 'an inner conviction of being overwhelmed by God'; if we have shared the experience which Charles Wesley was stammering to describe when he cried:

> O Thou who camest from above
> The pure celestial fire to impart,
> Kindle a flame of sacred love
> On the mean altar of my heart;

in other words, if we are sons and daughters of the authentic evangel, we will never rest until the new life we have found in Christ is the conscious possession of all mankind. Interest in the world crusade of Christianity thus stands in direct ratio to vitality of personal religion. In short, the missionary impetus is integral to conversion and the new birth, inherent in the experience of Christ, an immediate implicate of faith.

So it was with Paul at Damascus. The moment of reve-lation, which showed him that the Christ whom he had despised and rejected as crucified, dead and buried was in fact risen and alive by the power of God, gave him his com-mission—'The world must know! Necessity is laid upon me to publish this to the ends of the earth.' So it was with Matthew at Capernaum. Was not this the purpose of the feast by which he celebrated his conversion—to give his friends and associates, in meeting Christ, an opportunity to find what he had found and share the same redeeming blessing? It is said that when Rabbi Duncan was dying someone told him there was a man in the Infirmary, a foreign seaman, whose language no one could speak. 'I will learn it,' cried the scholar-saint, 'I will learn it that I may tell him of his Saviour!' When the everlasting mercy of Christ broke like a sudden dawn upon Saul Kane in Masefield's poem, it gave him his task in life:

> I knew that Christ had given me birth
> To brother all the souls on earth.

Whenever revival has visited the Church—as in the days of Francis of Assisi, or Zinzendorf and the Wesleys, or D. L. Moody and Henry Drummond—the missionary passion has been reborn.

Signs are not wanting of a new resurgence of such concern in many parts of the world to-day. It is all the more disquieting to observe that in some quarters missionary ardour has abated its force. One finds Christians who are depressed, inhibited, apathetic, and a Church crippled and immobile in its work overseas through lack of support. Many Church members have a totally defective sense of individual responsibility for the work to which their Church stands committed. They look on from the sidelines: they do not identify themselves with the stress and conflict of the arena. It has never dawned upon them that the one reason for the Church's existence is missionary. It is difficult to believe that we should have to hear the desperate annual financial appeals which have become so familiar if the cause of Christ were really the commanding interest of all who bear His name. And even among those who subscribe to missions there is often a lack of any consuming desire to share Christ personally with others. It is a sad reflection on the spiritual climate of the Western world that so often when members of the younger Churches of Africa and the East come into personal contact with us they express themselves as surprised and nonplussed by our lack of radiance and vitality and urgency and joy. 'Is this really the same religion,' they wonder, 'which broke on us like a rising dawn and filled our mouth with singing?' Thus we stand rebuked.

What are the reasons for this condition? Various factors suggest themselves.

One is that in many quarters *Christian conviction is haunted by the chilly shadow of intellectual doubt.* Can the faith hold up its head before the massive onset of secular science, and stand unintimidated before the incisive criticism of the logical positivist? Are the Christian facts still relevant in a blatantly non-christian world? This is the crucial question. Theological vagueness has begotten intellectual doubt, and intellectual doubt has begotten missionary apathy.

Another reason has been *self-distrust.* 'Who am I, and what is my people, that we should seek to thrust our beliefs upon others? Are we such a shining pattern of Christianity that we should presume to take upon ourselves the role of evangelist?' This difficulty is widely felt to-day; and indeed in a sense it is a sign of grace. Is the record of Christian nations so far above reproach that they can claim to be guides to peoples who have inherited another culture and an alien creed? A former generation sang:

> Can we, whose souls are lighted
>   With wisdom from on high,
> Can we to men benighted
>   The lamp of life deny?

But perhaps the representatives of Western civilisation have exploited the men benighted too long to use such words now with an easy conscience. Nor can we cavil at it if, having seen Christian nations locked in the deadly grapple of two barbarous wars, those benighted ones are sceptical of our wisdom and dubious of our light. There is a self-distrust which can progressively inhibit evangelising zeal and paralyse missionary endeavour.

It is probable that a third factor inhibiting missionary zeal to-day is to be found in *the break-up of the once familiar pattern of missionary enterprise.* In the era of Colonial expansion and prestige, it was felt by many in the Churches of the West to be a duty to bring Christianity to those for whom they were becoming responsible politically. But now with the shrinking of Colonial commitment on the one hand, and the appearance of indigenous Churches on the other, this duty has appeared to lose some of its compelling urgency. Eastern lands are claiming political independence; their Churches are doing the same—a process markedly stimulated by dislike of the bewildering divisions of Western Church life. More than this, resentment at Western domination has brought suspicion upon everything associated with Western culture, the Church included. In this new revolutionary situation, traditional patterns of evangelism are no longer adequate or even relevant. We have to face the fact that that particular era of missionary enterprise is closed. It is perhaps not surprising that this discovery has induced in some quarters an uneasy doubt and questioning about the whole future of the Church's mission.

But there is a fourth reason—and this by far the most serious. It is *assimilation to the world.* 'One reason,' wrote P. T. Forsyth, 'why the Church is too little missionary is that it is established on good terms with its world instead of being a foreign mission from another.' The powers of darkness will never be scattered by a Christendom infiltrated by the enemy; and a religion that is to redeem the perishing must itself be uncompromising in its allegiance to the Redeemer. Let there indeed be no misunderstanding here. The alternative to assimilation is not aloofness. Was Jesus aloof from publicans and sinners? The community of Jesus must be lovingly involved in all the life of men. But at the same time it must be recognisably a new creation. St. Paul in his day had to appeal to the Roman Christians not to be conformed to the world, but rather to be transformed by the renewing of their minds, for only to a Church radically different from the world will the world consent to listen; and the whole cause of the Kingdom of God, now as then, is at stake in that appeal.

III

TREASURE IN EARTHEN VESSELS

WE have seen various reasons why the Church is not getting its shoulder beneath the missionary burden Christ is carrying in the world to-day. On the Calvary road, Simon of Cyrene was conscripted to be the burden-bearer of the Lord; and too often the appeals for missionary giving have seemed as a summons to a conscript's task. But why should the word 'obligation' ever have to be heard in this connection? Surely the love of the forgiven, the gratitude of the redeemed, must shatter such legalistic notions and turn duty into privilege and joy. Sharing the Gospel and witnessing to Christ stand not upon a compulsive 'Thou shalt,' but upon a heartfelt 'Thank God I may!'

It follows that our primary need, if the Church is to be girded for its missionary task, is not more information or appeal, not better propaganda or more elaborate technique: it is *a deeper sense of the unsearchable riches of Christ*. Suppose you were a biological chemist, and found the cure for some disease which has scourged the human race, suppose that experiment proved it to be the long looked for, infallible remedy, would you hide that? It is against all the ethics of the kingdom of science to hold up any discovery that can alleviate the sufferings of humanity. And it is against all the ethics of the Kingdom of God to hold up the discovery of a Redeemer. Then why is it that this is precisely what we do so often? Can it be that we have not truly understood what prodigious incomparable wealth the Gospel holds? Can it be that we have been thinking of Christianity as an ideology to accept rather than as a Person to adore?

Jesus Himself spoke of the good news of the Kingdom as priceless treasure. He told of a poor labourer toiling in the fields, whose plough suddenly struck buried treasure. Picture the man careering wildly down the road, bursting in to the cottage where he lived, babbling incoherently till they wondered if he were mad, but getting out his news at last—'We are rich beyond the dreams of avarice!' This, said Jesus, is what it means to find the Kingdom. And this is the realisation which some of us Christians are needing desperately to recapture.

It is a tragedy that the Christian religion is in many minds identified merely with pious ethical behaviour and vague theistic belief, suffused with aesthetic emotionalism and a mild glow of humanitarian benevolence. This is not the faith which at the first awakened the world like a thousand trumpets, and made men feel it bliss in such a dawn to be alive. Men knew then what Christianity really was—the entrance into history of a force of immeasurable range, the lifting of human existence to a new level and a supernatural dimension, the imparting to men through Christ of the very life of God, even as the vine injects its very life into the branch. No wonder the New Testament throbs with excitement from end to end. No wonder Paul clamours and stammers about 'unsearchable riches' and 'unspeakable gifts'. It was this above everything else that made Paul himself a missionary and drove him tirelessly across the earth. The great frowning mountain ranges of Asia and the wide estranging seas were no barrier to this man, for beyond them were men dying without Christ. And still after nineteen hundred years all the springs of missionary power and passion are concentrated in these three words: 'Jesus, priceless treasure!'

Moreover, for our reinforcement let us reflect, as Paul himself reminded us, that *it is God's way to entrust the treasure to earthen vessels.* We have seen how self-distrust can inhibit personal evangelism and cripple the Church's mission. Who are we to convert the world? And no doubt, humanly speaking, it is frightfully incongruous that a priceless jewel should be enclosed in a box of clay, a lovely picture in a tawdry frame, a royal diadem in a cracked and dingy case in a museum thick with dust. Yet this is precisely the strategy of God. And there is a reason for the shattering discrepancy: the purpose, as Paul declared, is that the world should know that Christianity—all the triumphs of the faith in individual lives, and the onward march of the mission of the Church—is not to be explained by anything in man, any human virtue or prowess or ability (for, in the light of the men involved, any such explanation would be manifestly ludicrous and absurd); therefore the only possible explanation must be supernatural and divine. 'We have this treasure in earthen vessels, to show that the excellency of the power is of God and not of us.'

This is the answer to the disconsolate moods in which, looking at the Church and seeing its crippling, often stupid divisions, its bourgeois complacency, its failures pathetic enough to make the angels weep, we begin to ask—'Is this indeed the instrument of the mission of Christ? Is this to go out among the heathen as "the arm of Christ's strength, the tongue of Christ's Spirit, the visible token of Christ's presence"?' It is the answer also to the despairing moods in which we turn in upon ourselves: 'I the ambassador of this royal Jesus? I to wear the Christian name before the world? God pity me—poor earthen vessel—utterly unworthy!' This is the answer—that always it is upon human weakness and humiliation, not human strength and confidence, that God chooses to build His Kingdom; and that He can use us, not merely in spite of our ordinariness and helplessness and disqualifying infirmities, but precisely because of them. It is a thrilling discovery to make, and it can revolutionise our missionary outlook completely. For clearly, if this fact be true, the Church that believes it can be irresistible anywhere, and its mission for Christ against the powers of darkness becomes bright with an unquenchable hope; and the individual Christian who lives by it is undefeatable. Nothing can defeat a Church or a soul that takes, not its strength, but its weakness, and offers that to be God's weapon. It was the way of William Carey and Francis Xavier and Paul the apostle. 'Lord, here is my human weakness: I dedicate it to Thee for Thy glory!' This is the strategy to which there is no retort. This is the victory which overcomes the world.

IV

CHRIST THE KING

Up to this point, we have been considering one of the two fundamental factors in missionary motivation, namely, the constraint of Christ upon the individual life. We pass now to the other: *the kingship of Christ over history.*

I am strongly convinced that the whole future of the missionary enterprise is linked with, and depends on a right understanding of, the question of the relation of Jesus Christ to the historical process. Our missionary attitude will be largely conditioned by the answers we give to such questions as these: What did Jesus mean by the Kingdom of God, and what is its place in the context of secular history? Is Jesus King only of the Church, or is He King of the world as well? Is His Kingship real now, or potential in the future? Is there a new missionary urgency in the dangers of our contemporary situation? What is the ultimate goal of missions? Is it victory for Christ within the historical process, or is it victory beyond the consummation when history has ceased to be? Is it the gradual spread of the Gospel until the nations are at the feet of Jesus and the whole earth is Christianised? Or is it an apocalyptic act of God shattering time, abolishing history and bringing in eternity?

I suggest that the one satisfactory approach to these immensely important questions is along the line of *the New Testament proclamation of the Lordship of Christ.* All cramped and narrow notions of missionary motivation—all the planning and the strategy which are aimed simply at the rescuing of individual souls out of the clutches of the historical process and the corruption of the world—are far behind the insight of the New Testament Church when it fashioned its first creed in two words, like two sudden thrilling notes of a trumpet: *Kyrios Jesus*, Jesus is Lord.

It is upon God's mighty acts at the Cross and the Resurrection that Christ's Kingship stands for ever. When Pilate wrote upon the Cross 'This is the King', he had unconsciously expressed the divine determinate decree. 'He reigns from the tree.' This is the Gospel. It is not that we are sent out into the world to 'make Christ King'. How could it be that, when God has made Him King already and given Him the Name which is above every name? It is not that our missionary task is to co-operate with Jesus in seeking to establish the Kingdom, as though we were to prepare the way for its coming or work for its inauguration at some future day. How could it be that, when from every page of the Gospels the words and works of Jesus cry aloud that in Him the Kingdom has broken through and is now in the midst? It may indeed be a hidden Kingdom, with a King incognito, a mystery veiled from the eyes of sinful men and therefore unacknowledged.

> Concealed as yet this honour lies,
> By this dark world unknown,—
> A world that knew not when He came,
> Even God's eternal Son.

Nevertheless, He has taken hold upon history, and He is history's Lord.

Whenever we speak of an historical incarnation and of an objective atonement, we are asserting that God's mighty act in Christ has changed the human scene decisively and for ever even for those who do not believe on Him and who refuse to recognise His claim. The very earth which God has given to the sons of men has been different since the days when it was trodden by the feet of the one true Son of Man; and every human life, whether Christian or not, is affected by the cosmic battle fought out to a finish at Calvary between Jesus and the powers of darkness. In this sense He is King, not only of the Church, but of the universe itself.

Now there is all the difference in the world between going out on mission with the motive of helping Christ to become King, and going out because the King has sent you. If the dominical command were a summons to the Church to conduct a worldwide propaganda for Christ's enthronement, to dedicate its maximum resources to a herculean effort to bring His Kingdom in upon earth, it would indeed be a paralysing hopeless task. Sometimes the Church has in fact thought of its mission in those terms—and then the exhilaration has vanished from its spirit and the light has gone out of its face. Even to-day it is a not unfamiliar presentation of the missionary challenge. But basically it is quite alien to the New Testament. This was not the theology of missions on which the apostles launched out in that great age which saw the works of the Lord and His wonders in the deep. This would have been a frail makeshift raft, unfit for such a precarious voyage. What carried them through was the sure word of God that the kingly rule of heaven had broken right into history in Christ; that this Jesus was the royal dominion of God incarnate; and that the Lordship of Christ extended not merely to a group of disciples but to the nations of the earth, not to a few religious people but to all mankind, not to the Church alone but to the universe. 'Why do the heathen rage, and the people imagine a vain thing? I have set My King upon My holy hill of Zion. Ask of Me, and I shall give Thee the uttermost parts of the earth for Thy possession.' If the missionaries proclaimed this truth with passionate conviction, it was because not flesh and blood but God Himself had revealed it to them in the death and resurrection of His Son. And to-day it is no rhetorical wishful thinking but hard concrete fact we are expressing when we say:

> His Kingdom cannot fail;
> He rules o'er earth and heaven;
> The keys of death and hell
> Are to our Jesus given.

Now here we encounter one of the fundamental principles of a missionary theology. It is this—that *behind the imperative lies an indicative*. The Church must act, because God has acted already. The missionary cries, 'Necessity is laid upon me: woe is me if I preach not the Gospel,' because of certain historic unique unrepeatable events which have given him a Gospel to preach. The love of Christ constrains its ambassadors to suffer in history, because by that love history is already redeemed. The command 'Go ye into all the world' has behind it the urge and drive of that stupendous affirmation, 'All power has been given to Me in heaven and earth.' The dynamic of the Church's unaccomplished task is the accomplished deed of God. Underneath the urgent imperative there rests, firm as a rock, the eternal indicative.

V

REDEMPTION IN THREE TENSES

IT is important for our purpose to observe that within the New Testament itself the indicative of revelation, the act of God, appears in three distinct tenses.

Basically, it is *the past indicative* that carries the good news. What the apostles preached was neither a philosophy of life nor a theory of redemption. They preached events. They anchored their Gospel to history. They thrust upon their hearers' attention certain factual momentous occurrences precisely dated: 'in the fifteenth year of the reign of Tiberius Caesar', 'under Pontius Pilate', 'after three days'. 'This thing happened', they declared. 'Once and for all the Kingdom of heaven has broken in. Once and for all the Word has become flesh. Once and for all the powers of darkness have been defeated. God's deed stands towering over the wrecks of time, and against it you can batter all your doubts to pieces.' They wasted no time exhorting their hearers with moral homilies, or cajoling them with novel ideologies, or trying to build a Church on the shifting foundations of a man-centred constitution. They confronted them with something which had been done, and done by God for ever—one mighty act, decisive, final and complete.

> On Christ, the solid rock, I stand:
> All other ground is sinking sand.

But the missionary preaching of the apostles, starting as it did from this past indicative, did not stop there: it spoke also *in the present tense*. The great redemptive transaction was indeed complete, but it was not imprisoned in the past: it was contemporaneous. The revelation was dynamic and alive. God had raised up Christ—that was the accomplished fact; but it meant that Christ was living now, and who could measure the potentialities of this instant Presence for the Church or for the world? To be alive in the same world with the risen Christ—what a thrilling tension of expectancy this must involve, what a fresh unwearied wonder of discovery! Daily they were 'tasting', as one of them expressed it, 'the powers of the world to come'. The two ages had overlapped; time was shot through with eternity; and gleams of glory were continually piercing and scattering the darkness of sinful history. Earthen vessels though these men knew themselves to be, haunted even as Christians by the old Adam and appointed unto death, they nevertheless felt within themselves the throb of resurrection life. In union with the Second Adam, the 'Firstborn of a great brotherhood', they were finding their earthly existence permeated with unearthly meaning and laid hold upon by the Kingdom of God. Just as Jesus after the Resurrection had appeared to the disciples in His spiritual body, so now they in turn, though still bound by space and time and the shadow of death, knew that their mortal body was already being clothed upon with immortality. Paul, with a characteristically daring leap of faith, saw the Church as the expression of the spiritual yet corporeal presence of the Lord, the actual concrete organism of His continuing life, participating in His very being and interpenetrated by His love: in fact, as the Body of Christ.

Thus apostolic faith was never a mere tending of the sacred fire on the altar of a dead Galilean memory. Christ was not there. He was alive and present and in the midst. This is what differentiates a dynamic infectious faith from the dull tedium of conventional religion, and a living Church from a dead ecclesiastical machine. But it involves crisis too: 'this is the judgment, that light has come.' To Christ as Victor, all things in heaven and earth have been committed, not simply a select group of pious souls but the whole range and variety of human existence and indeed the universe itself; so that even where His Kingship is unrecognised or vehemently denied, that Kingship is a cosmic fact. Even when history appears a chaos, and the life of man subject to corruption and bedevilment, Christ's is the Kingdom, the power and the glory. In the Body of Christ, the historic incarnation becomes present fact. In every soul risen with Christ, the Resurrection is made contemporary. Through the witness of the redeemed the divine redeeming activity is continued. Both Church and world are Christ's; and to the fellowship of believers there can be no rest till every nation, every institution, every culture know and hail their Lord, and the world is at His feet.

Accordingly, there appears *the third tense of the apostles' Gospel*. It is conceivable that their double emphasis—on salvation as an accomplished fact, a decisive battle fought and won, and on the Kingdom as a contemporary reality, eternal life as a present possession—might have led them to minimise the future. This is in fact what has happened with certain modern theologies of the 'demythologising' school, whose existential emphasis has resulted in a virtual extrusion of the eschatological. What happened with the men of the New Testament was the exact reverse. Their insight taught them that if Easter was the culmination of the first Advent it was also the guarantee of the second. Knowing that the Kingdom had appeared in time and that Christ was reigning now, they turned to face the future with a new intensity of hope, a hope as certain as the promises of God. Realising that the decisive battle had been won, they flung themselves with magnificent abandon into the remaining toils and dangers of the campaign, sustained in all the hardships and dangers and persecutions of their mission by the certainty of the coming end, and straining their eyes through the darkness towards the final triumph of the Lord. Each Eucharist was a foretaste of the Messianic banquet and marriage supper of the Lamb.

Were they not right? You cannot be redeemed by Christ, and not be given in that very experience the revelation that it is God's purpose one day to sum up all things in Him. You cannot be a son of the Resurrection and not see all the world bathed in resurrection light. It is no utopian dream that underlies this hope but an irrefragable certainty, of which the title-deeds are already in faith's possession. When the New Testament speaks of the Holy Spirit as the 'earnest' or the 'first-fruits', the meaning is that in the new life imparted through Christ to the redeemed there has been anticipated and solidly guaranteed, as it were by a first sample or instalment, the end towards which God is leading the whole creation. As the writer to the Hebrews puts it, we have already 'tasted the powers of the world to come'. This miraculous thing, this life from the dead here and now, this supernatural presence and endowment to which all the saints have witnessed, and of which through the mercy of Christ even our own souls have had experience, is nothing less than the glory of the future consummation and the eternal world flashing its signals to us across the darkness of our sin-distorted present. In other words, to apprehend the Kingdom of God in time is to become aware that the Kingdom transcends time. To be redeemed by Christ is to see the cosmic plan unveiled: 'Then cometh the end, when He shall have delivered up the Kingdom to God, even the Father.'

We have seen, then, that in the mission proclamation of the Church all three tenses, past, present and future, meet and interlock. This fact—let us notice in passing—is *focused significantly in the two great Sacraments* which the Christian mission has always carried as its banners through the world.

Baptism in the New Testament is so much more than a simple rite of dedication. It is an act of God. It is a threefold act of God's eternal love. It looks back to the past, to the accomplished work of Christ, who spoke of His sufferings and death as His own baptism for the sins of the world: so that to be baptised means, in the deepest and most spiritual sense, to be sealed with the sign of the Cross. Further, it signifies in the present God's incorporation of the individual into the Body of Christ, so that daily henceforth the life of the Christian is nourished and sustained by participation in the life of Christ. And finally it points forward to the future, for in this divine electing act we are 'sealed with the Holy Spirit of promise, the earnest of our inheritance'; so that baptism into the Church militant is always prophetic of the life of the Church triumphant.

So also with the other banner of the faith, *the Lord's Supper*. It is a sadly mutilated doctrine of the Lord's Supper that results when any one of the three tenses interacting in the Sacrament is ignored. Here the Church remembers the upper room and the passion of the Lord and the night in which He was betrayed. But to make the Eucharist a memorial feast and nothing more is to imprison it in the past and terribly to impoverish its true nature. For here to the gathered Church the Christ of Easter comes again, King and living Lord, in intimate present communion, bringing gifts of cleansing and forgiveness. And here, finally, is prefigured the Messianic banquet at the end, when according to His own promise the victory shall be complete and He shall sit down with His people in the Kingdom of God.

VI

INDICATIVE AND IMPERATIVE

In all three tenses, then, the apostles proclaimed the great indicative of God's action in history and in the lives of men. 'This has God done. This is God doing. This shall God do at the end.'

Now comes the crucial point. *Always this basic indicative contains at its heart a veiled imperative. And always at the heart of the imperative is a missionary challenge.* 'All power has been given to Me in heaven and earth. *Go ye therefore!*' 'Love so amazing, so divine, *demands*'—everything we have to offer. The gift of the Spirit brings the task. Election means service.

It is vitally important that these two moods of the Gospel —the indicative and the imperative—should be held in due balance and proportion. Failure to do this can gravely weaken the impact of Christendom upon the world. There have been periods in the Church's history when this has happened, and serious damage to the missionary cause has resulted. And still to-day there are Christians who mistakenly resolve the tension between the two moods by concentrating on one to the exclusion of the other. What God has joined together man has put asunder.

On the one hand, *there are those who, hearing the indicative of the Gospel, fail to catch the imperative.* God has acted. The mighty deed of salvation is achieved. In due season God will gather His Kingdom to Himself. That, for them, is everything. Nothing remains to be done. The one thing needful is to possess God, to dwell in the secret place of the Most High, to cultivate the interior devotional life and aim at personal holiness.

These are the Quietists. Of course, there is a tremendous element of truth in this position. It is emphatically true that the one foundation of hope for the world is the Rock of Ages. We owe everything to the *opus operatum* of the Lord, the finished work of Christ.

But this position can so easily degenerate into a sentimental unchristlike irrelevance, concentrating on its own spiritual culture and taking far too little cognisance of the sin entrenched within society and of the vast agonies and miseries of men. It is most unfortunate that Luther's Reformation doctrine of the two realms has sometimes been misinterpreted in this way in post-Reformation thought and practice. A Church that is content to remain isolated in sanctified seclusion from the world around its doors and the clamorous problems of the age has no right to bear the name of Him who chose to dwell with publicans and sinners. It has no word to speak that the unbeliever can understand. It tends to draw in upon itself, more concerned to maintain its own institutional life than to break down barriers by offering the outsider friendship in the name of Christ. Small wonder if the world passes by that kind of Church with a shrug of contempt. It has ceased to be Messianic. It has disowned its redemptive mission. To this travesty of the Gospel Christ's eyes are as a flame of fire.

On the other hand, *there are those who hear clearly the imperative of service, but are hazy about or unmindful of the indicative on which it is based.* They are so vividly conscious of the demand to be up and doing for the salvation of this atrociously needy world that they can scarce tarry to consider what God has done once for all. Their New Jerusalem is a future Utopia to be achieved by toil and tears and sweat and blood, not a gift which has already appeared in the midst of time in Jesus Christ.

These are the Activists. They are not far from the Kingdom of God. Jesus, looking upon them, loves them. Without doubt there is an element of true nobility in this attitude. It may depreciate creeds and dogmas, but it does care mightily for men and women. It may be weak theologically and vague about the meaning of worship; but it is a standing rebuke to any isolated self-centred Church.

Nevertheless, noble as it is, it bears within itself the seeds of its own disillusionment. It cannot quite throw off the haunting suspicion that the best New Jerusalem built by man's endeavour will fail to satisfy that nameless longing of the human spirit for something better than improved communities and garden cities, that cry of the pilgrim generations for 'a city which hath foundations, whose builder and maker is God'.

It is significant that the greatest rival of the Christian mission to-day—an atheistic ideology centring in a revolutionary imperative—has in its own way recognised the need to base the imperative of demand on a prior indicative of doctrine. Communism owes its spectacular triumphs partly at least to the fact that the masterful imperative of world revolution appeals to a deep if untutored instinct of the human heart. So militant and totalitarian has become this imperative of Communism that it has trampled the divine indicative underfoot. But the significant thing is that even Communism seems to be aware that some indicative must be found or invented to sustain and justify its missionary imperative. If the indicative of the divine action in history is contemptuously cast out, the indicative of dialectical materialism must be brought in. If the mighty, determining acts of God are fiercely and furiously denied, there must be established the determinism of the logic of events irresistibly carrying the revolution to its goal. In other words, even the Communist has discovered that no missionary imperative can stand which is not solidly founded on an indicative. How much more confidently must the Christian maintain this truth—the Christian whose passion for the redemption of the world is based upon the action of God in Christ by which the world has once for ever been redeemed!

VII

WHAT GOD HAS JOINED TOGETHER

IT may be helpful at this point to illustrate the two defective and one-sided positions on the missionary question which we have been considering, by reference to one story in the Gospels in which both are mirrored.

'Let us build three tabernacles,' said Peter and his fellow-disciples on the Mount of Transfiguration. 'Let us perpetuate the beatific vision, and forget the fever and the fret down yonder in the valley where men sit and hear each other groan. Why break our hearts on the stony recalcitrance of Galilee or on the Via Dolorosa of Jerusalem, when there is this encompassing glory, this mystic communion so richly to enjoy'? It is to this mood, which has been in many an age the Church's temptation, that the Master's word rings out clear: 'Come back to earth! Here is this clamorous desperate human situation—come right back into it! What God has joined together put not asunder.' And if Peter, James and John hesitate, if the Church demurs, on Christ goes without it, striding down the hill to where the need of man is greatest: for He cannot stay out of it.

But perhaps it is the other mistake mirrored in this story, the opposite kind of blunder, into which to-day we are more apt to fall: not the mistake of the three disciples on the mountain, but the mistake of the remaining nine at its foot. What they were trying to do, in their Master's absence, was to perform in their own strength a miracle of healing on a poor delirious demon-possessed creature in whom the anguish of the world seemed typified. Jesus had vanished. He was up among the clouds. There was no saying when He might return. But what matter? Were they not practical men, with skill, initiative, ingenuity? Wait upon the Lord? Why should they? Were not realism and rational planning better for a revolutionary situation than idealism and the supernatural? 'Let us go ahead! We will exorcise this devil successfully.' But they were discomfited. Still the tragedy in the valley dragged on—the plight of the demented patient and his distracted father unrelieved. Still the quizzical bystanders taunted and badgered these nine men, that nucleus of a Church, with their failure. And in the end it took the majesty of Jesus, descending from the mountain, to master the misery of the valley. 'Why could we not do it?' is the perennial question. And still the Church gets its answer: 'This kind goeth not forth but by prayer and fasting.'

We have seen, then, how in these two one-sided positions, the quietist and the activist, the indicative and the imperative of the Gospel tend to fall apart. What God has joined together the Church has put asunder. It may not therefore be out of place to adduce another New Testament story—one of the greatest missionary stories in the world—in which very dramatically the two moods coalesce. Peter on the Transfiguration Mountain in the Gospel becomes now Peter on the housetop in the Acts. Again there are the vision and the voice from heaven; then suddenly, shattering his reverie, the loud knocking at the door beneath. It was the Gentile world, in the persons of Cornelius' men, clamouring for Christ. It was the Gospel in its weakness being summoned forth to face the arena of fierce racial clash and conflict. We ought to ponder well the tension of that moment, when both sounds were ringing in Peter's ears at once—the voice of God above, and the knock at the door below. For this, at any given moment of history, is the crisis of the Church, standing always between the housetop and the door, between revelation and mission, between the deed of God and the demand of men, between Christ the Redeemer and Cornelius crying to be redeemed. Peter, out on the dangerous, incalculable road to Caesarea and the Gentiles, with his spirit still bathed in the afterglow of the housetop, still vibrant from communion with the high God of his salvation—here is the true essential union of mystic vision and missionary passion. And, for our heartening, let it not be forgotten that when Peter reached Caesarea he found that Someone Else had been there before him; and so there dawned upon him the realisation that it had not been only Cornelius' soldiers who had come to his gate that day and rudely interrupted his vision. The disturbing voice had been the voice of Christ Himself: 'Behold, I stand at the door and knock.'

Let us go forth therefore unto Him outside the camp.

VIII

CREED AND REVOLUTION

THE imperative of the Church's mission to the world is firmly based on the indicative of God's deed in Christ. I wish now to carry the argument a stage further and to suggest that every single article of the faith, each separate consecutive statement of the creed, is of this kind—an indicative holding at its heart a missionary imperative.

Thus the statement '*I believe in God the Father*' looks simple and straightforward enough. Nevertheless, its implications are drastic to the point of being positively frightening. For veiled beneath the comforting indicative of the divine Fatherhood lies the inexorable imperative of human brotherhood. 'Our Father?' Then we belong to the family. In giving us Himself, God gives us our brothers and sisters of this earth. Thus in the very moment when we confess the eternal Fatherhood, our racial, social, economic policies are searched and judged. More than that (for here as elsewhere judgment must begin at the House of God) our ecclesiastical jealousies, our failures in humility, our minimising of traditions other than our own, our denigrating of others' grace, our dreary, petty standardisation, our pathetic spiritual complacency, our habit of tracing the sinfulness of disunity to others' stubbornness rather than to our own—all this is seen to be, as Paul expressed it bluntly, 'sheer carnality', the very stuff of sin; or as John put it in even graver language, by these things 'we make God a liar'. 'One is your Father,' said Jesus. This is the indicative of revelation, out of whose fathomless depths there immediately springs the imperative of mission: 'See that ye live as brethren.'

Or take the creed on the Incarnation. '*He was made man.*' '*The Word was made flesh.*' '*Born of the Virgin Mary, suffered under Pontius Pilate.*' Here is the indicative of the divine involvement in history, this unlimited self-identification of Jesus with the sinners He had come to save. Their burden was His burden, their suffering His suffering, their valley of the shadow of death His chosen pilgrim road. When He took 'Son of Man' as His favourite self-designation, one part at least of the meaning was this constraint to give Himself utterly to the race of men. But—and this is the point—we have no right to accept the comfort of this truth and evade its overwhelming challenge. If with the New Testament we believe that the eternal Word took upon Himself a body of flesh, we have no right to preach a disembodied Gospel dissociated from material and mundane concerns. The indicative of the incarnation carries with it a revolutionary imperative. It implicates us inextricably in history. It compels us to see the circumstances of man's corporate life as the raw materials of God's eternal purpose. The mysticism which would bypass earthly conditions it brands as a nauseating irrelevance. 'As the Father sent Me into the world,' said Jesus to His men, 'so send I you.'

But let no man nor Church be under any illusion as to what obedience to this imperative involves: for whether at home or beyond the seas, the integration of religion and history, of mission and life, of evangelism and social concern, will always occasion misunderstanding, offence, even furious opposition; this is 'the reproach of Christ' for which Christians must be prepared. Too often we have allowed the faith to appear as a reactionary influence in a revolutionary world. It has seemed to be in league with the existing order against the ferment of ideas and the seismic upheaval of the age. Men have come to regard it has having a vested interest in the maintenance of the *status quo*. The truth is the exact reverse. It is the world that pursues its dull undeviating way, its monotonous cyclic rhythm of war and peace, hope and disillusionment, utopian freedom and totalitarian enslavement: it is Christianity that is the revolution. It is secular ideals which are 'the opiate of the people': it is the word of the Lord which is a two-edged sword. How could it be otherwise, seeing that the Christian faith had its origin in the most revolutionary event in history, the Resurrection of Jesus?

Of those whose religious experience has meant the pleasant comfort and security of having a solid rock beneath their feet, not all have realised that the rock is volcanic, and that sleeping volcanoes can awake. Long ago at Thessalonica the objection urged against the Gospel was that it 'turned the world upside down'; and still wherever the Gospel comes, the authentic Gospel—in India and Africa, in Britain and America—the same revolutionary force is unleashed; which is a main reason why reactionary elements, interested in the conservation of settled conditions, view with intense disfavour the indiscriminate propagation of a faith so essentially volcanic, declaring that 'missions spoil the native', that evangelism disturbs the even tenour of our ecclesiastical way. 'The Gospel is a new factor of immense potency,' writes Bishop Stephen Neill. 'It cannot but tear the seamless robe of the established order. The missionary, whether he knows it or not, comes inevitably as a destroyer.' This is true in the sense that the proclamation of Christ lays the axe to the roots of the tree of serfdom and superstition, of racial discrimination and social injustice. From the hour when the Word became incarnate and the love of heaven struck down into the plagues and confusions of the world, the Church received the marching-orders of its mission. Like its Master, it was to take upon itself the burden of the plight of men, and to involve itself in all the conditions of their life on earth.

From that warfare there is no discharge, from that concern of love no possible release, until God is all in all.

One further statement of the creed let me take by way of illustration, before passing from this stage of the argument. *'From thence'* [the right hand of God] *'He shall come to judge the quick and the dead.'* This is the affirmation of the Church's Advent hope. This is the confidence of the divine consummation at the end of the age. If Jesus is Son of Man as being involved in the tears and tragedies of history, He is also Son of Man as apocalyptic transcendent Redeemer. If in the Valley of Humiliation He met and routed the powers of darkness, this itself is proof that He shall come in glory at the last to gather His Kingdom to Himself. But here again at the very heart of the sublime indicative lies the concealed imperative. For what is the meaning of the interval of grace which God has granted to mankind, what is the purpose of the intermediate period between the victory of the Cross and the Resurrection and the crowning triumph at the end, what but this—'The Gospel must first be published among all nations'? 'All power is given to Me in heaven and earth. Go ye therefore!' The present age, by the fiat of God Himself, is to be characterised as *the era of mission*, in which every Christian is implicated. It is as though the Lord of Calvary and Easter said: 'I hold all history in the hollow of My hand; but I will not wind up the scroll nor cut it short in righteousness until all men have been given the opportunity of sharing with Me in My victory.'

Here, then, is the imperative of the Church's mission. Here is the urgency of the unfinished task. By the decree of God, it is the missionary preaching of the Gospel that is to fill and span the interval between the first and the second Advents, between the Cross and the Resurrection on the one side and the Parousia on the other; or, as Cullmann puts it, between the decisive battle which has already taken place and the final Victory Day that will end the campaign. It was the clear realisation of this stupendous fact that explains the immense verve and lustre and excitement of apostolic Christianity. It was this overwhelming sense of a summons to share in the divine redemptive plan that made those men of the early mission stronger than the legions of Rome. And to-day we should lay it well to heart that when the risen Christ, in the last words of the Gospel record, gave the Church final instructions for its journey across history to the second Advent and sent it out upon that long incalculable pilgrimage, the promise He then added—'Lo, I am with you alway, even unto the end of the world'—was not unconditional. It was firmly placed in a missionary setting. Only in connection with missionary fidelity is the promise valid. Christ will not remain in the midst of a Church that neglects its missionary calling, nor continue to grant His presence to a Christian who shelves responsibility for evangelism. The condition of possessing Christ within is obedience to the missionary imperative without. Only a truly Messianic society can know His communion who is Messiah and Lord, and do His works until He come.

To sum up this stage in the argument. There is, I submit, ample evidence for the assertion that every single article of the creed is an implicit imperative, pointing straight at the Church's mission. By every separate 'I believe' which we take upon our lips, we stand self-committed. How pathetically inadequate, then, is the view which regards missions as one activity amongst others in the Christian programme, and interest in missions as an option, an extra, to be taken up or not according to the whim or preference of the individual Church member! The fact that missionary societies have often represented a minority movement within the Church betokens a woeful misunderstanding both of the nature of the Gospel and of the function of the Church as the new

Israel of God. How can anyone say: 'I live, yet not I, but Christ liveth in me,' and not know himself implicated in Christ's redemptive purpose on the earth? How can any Church claim to be the true Israel, the Body of Christ, and not be passionately missionary?

IX

THE MEANING OF HISTORY

At this point there comes into sight another fundamental affirmation of a missionary theology. If it affirms, as I have endeavoured to show, that the missionary imperative for the Church springs out of the redemptive indicative of the divine action in history, past, present and to come, it also affirms that *the total meaning of history is the universal reign of Christ.*

To this indeed the whole Biblical revelation bears witness. As the new Israel, the true Messianic society, the Church is God's chosen instrument for the ultimate redemption of humanity. This is the core of the doctrine of election—this prophetic insight that salvation is no private affair, this recognition and acceptance of a missionary destiny.

Already in the Old Testament, it is the missionary motive that underlies the election of Israel. If at many points in the Old Testament the chosen people of the covenant appear to be God's exclusive interest, if sometimes the work of providence seems focused upon a still narrower group, the Remnant, this is simply the expression of the divine strategy which aims at the ultimate penetration of all nations through a people saved by the Lord. In the last resort, the Remnant itself is narrowed down to a single point, the Son of Man, the Saviour of the world, from whose death and resurrection there springs a reconstituted Israel, the people of the new covenant, the apostolic missionary Church. Thus the purpose of God in history, hidden at the first but subsequently revealed—as Paul puts it, 'the mystery which was kept secret since the world began but now is made manifest'—has never been anything other than a missionary passion. And the crowning day when the divine work shall be accomplished and the Church's mission shall be complete, when there shall be no more Jew nor Greek, barbarian, Scythian, bond nor free, but all shall be one in Christ—this was the goal God had in view from the day when He called Israel out of Egypt, and indeed from the first dawn of human history and the making of the world.

No doubt there was many an hour in the history of Israel —as there has been in the history of the Church—when the missionary reason for its existence was forgotten or disowned. No doubt national prejudices hardened the Jewish heart and narrow horizons blocked its vision. Yet God's first missionary command to Abraham—'Get thee out'—rings all the way from Genesis to John the Baptist. The pillar of cloud and fire before the host of Israel moves steadily onward. Ever and again through the battle-haze of Israel's wars and the thick night of her sins there comes a glimpse of a Church on the march—in the exodus, in the prophetic revivals, in the agony of defeat, in the spiritual discoveries of the captivity, in the return of the exiles, in the dreams of the apocalyptists, in the high courage of the Maccabean martyrs. The passages in which this vision of a marching, missionary Church comes to expression are amongst the most thrilling in the Old Testament. 'In that day shall five cities in the land of Egypt speak the language of Canaan, and swear loyalty to the Lord of hosts. In that day shall there be a highway out of Egypt to Assyria. In that day shall Israel be the third with Egypt and with Assyria, even a blessing in the midst of the land: whom the Lord of hosts shall bless, saying, Blessed be Egypt My people, and Assyria the work of My hands, and Israel Mine inheritance.'

Always when Israel was becoming lethargic and static and self-contained, losing the evangelising zeal and the eschatological hope, turning in upon itself through paralysing fear of the welter of Assyrian and Babylonian paganism and idolatry, always there would come the trumpet-note, 'Get ye out! This is not your rest, this bivouac in the wilderness —not this, but a city out of sight, into which you are to bring all nations as a tribute to the Lord.' There was a man of God who in his dreams heard Zion rejoicing in its Messiah and the daughter of Jerusalem shouting Hosannas to her King; and this, he noted, was to be the characteristic mark of Messiah's Advent—'He shall speak peace unto the heathen. His dominion shall be from sea to sea, and from the river to the ends of the earth.' All history would be gathered up in His universal reign.

When Jesus on Palm Sunday made that prophecy His own, the seal was set to the Church's universal task. Often throughout its story the new Israel, like the older prototype, has turned in upon itself and betrayed its missionary charter and grown tired of the long crusade. Often it has been content to stand on the defensive, fortifying its battlements against the besieging pressure of an alien world. Often the faith has become rigid, conventional, immobile. But the same Providence that sent the prophets to resurrect the dry bones of Israel's dead complacency into an exceeding great army, a missionary host upon the march, has broken again in every time of revival into the Church, summoning it forth from behind its barriers and thrusting it out into an indifferent or hostile age to Christianise the world's life and to reclaim the wilderness for the Redeemer. 'Let us go forth unto Him outside the camp'—*unto Him*, mark you, for since the day when He suffered outside the gate it is out on the roads to that alien world that Jesus is most surely to be found, and to stay in the camp is to lose Him. Whenever the Spirit of Christ has come mightily upon the Church, the missionary passion has been reborn. For the true Messianic society is never a static encampment, but always an army on the march—

> On, to the bound of the waste,
> On, to the City of God.

X

WORLD CHURCH AND LOCAL PARISH

THIS prompts two further reflections. The first bears on the ecumenical issue, the second on the life of the individual congregation.

On the one hand, is it not clear that *the concern for unity in the Church and the concern for mission stand and fall together?* There have grown up two great movements, the International Missionary Council and the World Council of Churches, the former dedicated originally to world evangelism, the latter to the quest of Christian unity. But basically and inescapably the two concerns are one. For the more fully the Church becomes united, the more truly is it the Body of Christ; and the more truly it is the Body of Christ, the more essentially missionary must be its spirit. The opposite is also true. The more the Church tolerates partisan, divisive and competitive elements, the more it distorts its witness and frustrates the missionary purpose of its existence. If there is a denominational loyalty that is large-minded and noble, there is also an obdurate sectarianism that is petty and intolerable. It is one of the most hopeful signs of the times that this essential nexus between mission and unity is now being realised, and action taken accordingly—even although there may be certain sections and movements within the Church that continue to ignore it or even to oppose it.

In this matter it is the younger Churches which are speaking with the most unequivocal voice and applying the strongest pressure, and surely they have the mind of Christ. Surely it is manifest that it would be as wrong and futile to strive after organisational unity among the Churches while ignoring missionary obligation as it would be to plant missions here, there and everywhere without a single thought of the upbuilding of the new communities into the Body of Christ. It was our Lord Himself who made this indissoluble bond between mission and unity clear once for all when, having prayed 'that they all may be one', He added immediately 'in order that the world may believe.'

The other reflection concerns the life of the individual congregation. It is this: *a thoroughgoing emphasis on the essentially missionary nature of the Church will reorientate all our parish activity*. Every congregation ought to be prepared periodically to re-examine its own organisational life in the light of its one basic task, and to jettison or radically transform any of its activities which do not helpfully contribute to the central purpose. Christ's warfare in the world to-day is too critical and demanding to permit the squandering of time and effort on anything that is irrelevant to His campaign or a drag upon His mission. 'Take it away! Why cumbereth it the ground?'

In particular, it must be made abundantly clear that it is the layman who holds the key to the situation. The hope of the Church to-day lies not in any ecclesiastical strategy or clerical professionalism but in a really vigorous movement of lay religion. Never let us forget that it was not as a hierarchy, it was as a layman's movement, that the Christian religion began; and one of the most urgent tasks of the hour is to fashion new channels through which the apostolate of the laity may find full and vital expression. For every Church is called to be a society of witness, every Church member is in the front line of the battle; and the priesthood of all believers, so dear to our Reformation faith, is a fact the vast potency of which still waits to be discovered.

Even our traditional modes of worship need to be brought under the searchlight of the consuming fire of Jesus' missionary passion. Why do we go to Church? What are we hoping for from our attendance there? 'Our feet shall stand within thy gates, O Jerusalem.' Wherein lies this mysterious constraint? 'If I forget thee, O Jerusalem, let my right hand forget its cunning.' Do we come to Church to be refreshed in our own spiritual life? Is it to be reassured and comforted against a horde of besieging doubts and fears? Is it to escape from the wilderness of the world into an oasis of recollection and peace? All this, certainly. But if it is truly in Christ's name we are worshipping, something else must be happening as well. We are being challenged. We are being disturbed. We are being burnt by the flame of Christ's terrible compassion for all the sheep without a shepherd. Our hope that the Church might be to us a haven of a little private spiritual security is rudely shattered.

If Christ is really present in a service—I mean, not merely being spoken of in worship as a third party who is somewhere else, but actually there in the midst—then something of the travail of His great heart over a perishing world is present too. Without this, Churchgoing can become a mere pious indulgence, and all the round of congregational activity intolerably trite and petty. If our congregational life ever becomes an end in itself, if we become introverted ecclesiastically and satisfied in our introversion, if our horizon is this society of ours, this building, this minister and people, this particular spiritual family circle, we are on the road to perdition. A hard saying, undoubtedly, but true; for where Christ comes to His own, always it is to redeem their worship from spiritual self-centredness, always to thrust them out in loving service for the men He died to save. There is a prayer of Asa King of Judah on the eve of a great battle, which memorably expresses the spirit of true worship. 'O Lord our God, we rest on Thee; and in Thy name we go against this multitude.' To come to rest in the Most High, and then in the strength of that experience to go out against the powers of darkness in the battle for the Kingdom of the Lord—this is essential worship. This is the true missionary Church, 'fair as the moon, clear as the sun, and terrible as an army with banners'.

XI

THE PRESENT PROSPECT

Two vitally important questions remain. *What are the present prospects for missions? What is the ultimate goal?*

Jesus in a dark day told His disciples that if they could interpret the signs of the times they might discover that *the most menacing catastrophic human situations were charged with divine potency and betokened a new day of the Son of Man.* Is this not true of the crisis in which we stand to-day?

In one view, the missionary prospect is daunting and disquieting indeed. Frustration meets us everywhere. In Asia and the Far East, doors which once stood wide open have been slammed in the face of the heralds of the Cross. Barricades which appeared to be collapsing before the Christian advance have been re-erected and consolidated. Ought we not therefore to soft-pedal the missionary appeal until the times are more propitious? This might seem the prudent policy. 'Wait till the skies clear. It is absurd to talk about advance when in so many lands Christ has His back to the wall, and the very existence of His Church is at stake. Nor is it expedient, coming nearer home, to press urgent missionary demands upon people whose minds are preoccupied and distracted with grim, besieging problems round their own doors. The stony ground of bewilderment and confusion is no good soil for the producing of a spiritual harvest. You will never have men taking the Kingdom of heaven by storm in an age that has witnessed hell let loose upon the earth. Put that mad hope away!'

It is an understandable attitude, no doubt. It is a common-

sense attitude. The disciples who, seeing the hungry multitude milling around, said to Jesus 'Send them away' were
being eminently reasonable. They had accurately assessed a
most embarrassing situation. There will never be any lack
of arguments—eminently reasonable arguments—for thrusting aside the immediate responsibility of mission and sending
the multitude away. The arguments from the unpropitious
nature of the time are shouting loud at us to-day. But one
thing is certain. It is precisely this kind of spirit that the
Bible on every page challenges and rebukes. And if we are
living to-day in an apocalyptic age, as we undoubtedly are,
nothing surely is more vitally important for the missionary
cause than that we should recapture and seek to make our
own the profound Biblical insight into history, and into the
inner significance of the shattering events by which the lives
of men and nations are conditioned.

What is this insight? The men of the Bible are far away
beyond such a reading of history as that which Matthew
Arnold gave in haunting words:

> We are here as on a darkling plain
> Swept with confused alarms of struggle and fight,
> Where ignorant armies clash by night.

The men of the Bible know and declare that if the powers of
darkness have a lot of rope nevertheless the end of the rope
is in the hands of God. They see that God in His sovereignty
can use even what is pagan and demonic as the agent of His
purifying judgment upon Israel and the Church. They
understand that Nebuchadnezzar, Sennacherib, Antiochus,
Caesar are unconscious instruments of an eternal providence.
They proclaim that 'the earth is the Lord's and the fulness
thereof'; and that even if the world seems sometimes to be
careering to the devil God still holds the reins, and His
purpose shall not fail.

Thus *judgment and hope* are the twin perspectives of the

Biblical insight into history. In these two contexts stands Israel's mission to the world.

Can we not make this insight our own to-day, when the very life of the Christian mission is being challenged by dark forces that bestride the world with their idolatry? Perhaps we have been inclined in our thinking to fix upon the idolatry of the forces of aggression, and have failed sufficiently to consider that they may conceivably represent *a judgment on Christendom for all that Christendom has left undone*. The very word 'crisis' means judgment; and we are certainly failing to hear what God the Lord is saying to us in our present critical situation if we denounce the idolatry of the demonic forces without recognising the judgment which through their instrumentality God is bringing in upon those who bear His name.

Thus, for example, it is no adequate reaction to the menace of the times to preach Christianity as a barren anti-Communism, and to make this the mission of the Church. The first essential response to the judgments of God is penitence. Must we not repent when it is borne in upon us that too often in the past our 'disembodied' gospels, our otherworldly complacencies, our ostracism of prophetic voices in the Church daring to propound a more revolutionary Christianity, our corporate involvement in racial and social injustices, have helped to create the very climate and soil in which anti-religious forces most readily breed and grow? 'It can well be,' writes Father A. G. Hebert, 'that the Marxism that we know would never have arisen if Christians in the age of the Industrial Revolution had not exploited the poor, identified their Christianity with the privilege of a particular class and failed to realise that Communism which is demanded by the truth of the mystical Body of Christ.' By all means let Christendom condemn idolatry and denounce aggression; but let it first recognise the judgment of the Lord and perform works meet for repentance.

It is at this point that the other perspective in the Biblical insight into history begins to appear. At the heart of inexorable judgment it proclaims *indomitable hope*. For ultimately the demonism of Pharaoh and Nebuchadnezzar and Caesar is self-destructive. The idolatrous force, which becomes the unwitting instrument of an inscrutable providence, is shattered and cast away. And if the prophets of Israel could thus defy despair, how much more should we give the lie to that dull hopelessness which has settled down on many minds to-day—we who in the Resurrection of Christ have seen the divine determination to make righteousness prevail!

'This is no time for missions'—so it is said. The fact is that never was there an hour when the burning urgency of the missionary enterprise was more apparent. A Christendom baptised under the judgments of God into a spirit of contrition, penitent of its remoteness from the miseries of men, penitent also of its own sinful divisions, and going forth now not as the ambassador of Western culture but as the bearer of the compassion and the charity of Christ, can face a thousand difficulties undaunted, with this as the song of its march:

> Awake, our souls! Away, our fears!
> Let every trembling thought be gone!

If the Biblical reading of history has any relevance to-day, it means that this present cataclysmic hour is alive with spiritual potentialities. God's judgments are in fact God's mercy. Have not our own eyes seen signs of this? Did not the late Archbishop Temple characterise the emergence in this war-torn generation of a world Church as the great new fact of the age? Is not the Church to-day astride many of the most decisive highways of the world? Where there is a global strategy, retreat at one point may be matched by dramatic advance elsewhere. It is recorded in the Acts of the

Apostles that when a sudden ruthless persecution was let loose on the Jerusalem Church 'they that were scattered abroad went everywhere preaching the word'; and the result of that compulsory evacuation was the outbreak of a great revival throughout the length and breadth of Samaria. Jesus Himself told His disciples that the familiar depressing adage about having to wait long months for harvest was more than half a lie: 'Lift up your eyes, and look on the fields, for they are white already to harvest.' And even as He spoke, as if in dramatic corroboration of His words, the road which had stood bare and deserted in the shimmering heat was suddenly filled with hurrying crowds eagerly thronging out to meet the new Messiah.

This is, in fact, our situation to-day. To take just one illustration—there is the worldwide hunger for literacy which Dr Frank Laubach has stressed so vividly. Have we grasped the possibilities of the extraordinary fact that ten million illiterates are now learning to read each year? If the forces of Christianity do not take this tide at the flood, Christ's enemies certainly will. Never before in history have Christian literature and Christian witness had such exciting opportunities. Never before has there been such a chance of bringing millions to Christ. This is our present situation. How long the opportunity may remain we cannot tell. It may be frighteningly short. But for the moment the door is wide open. What can this mean but that God's judgment is fraught with mercy, and chaos with creative hope? Well for us if through the crash and tumult of the breaking of nations we can hear the prophetic voice—'God is working His purpose out. This is the way to a new day of the Lord. Lift up your hearts! Your redemption draweth nigh.'

XII

THE ULTIMATE GOAL

So we reach our final question. From the present prospects of missions we turn to *the ultimate goal*. What are we hoping for in the end from the missionary enterprise? What has the Church been aiming at all these years? Is it the triumph of the Gospel within the historical process? Is it the complete irreversible Christianisation of every people and culture throughout the earth? Is it a rising crescendo of doxology till all the voices of the universe ring out Christ's praise alone? Is it the worldwide acknowledgment of Jesus

> where'er the sun
> Doth his successive journeys run?

Or, alternatively, is it a goal beyond history altogether? Are we to accept it that history as such is irredeemable, and that there is no goal short of the consummation in the world unseen when the earth and all its works have vanished and time shall be no more?

These questions have a vital bearing on the global strategy of Christendom. In any pilgrimage it is important to be clear about the goal; and this holds good emphatically of the mission of the pilgrim Church. Where are we tending in our march? Is it to a world progressively evangelised, a society purged finally of every evil, a brotherhood of nations united for ever at the feet of Christ? Or is it to the shattering of history, the dissolution of the kingdoms of the world, and the apocalypse of eternity?

Two views contend for mastery.

The apocalyptic outlook would dismiss the dream of the emergence of a perfectly Christianised society as a dangerous delusion. Its attitude towards the spatio-temporal structure of existence is fundamentally pessimistic. Here, it is maintained, no final victory is attainable. God's word to the Israel of the exodus—'The Egyptians whom ye have seen this day, ye shall see no more again for ever'—cannot be applied to man's hope of a new exodus in history from the bondage of corruption and frustration. Our Egyptians are more tough and obdurate and resilient. The multi-headed hydra of Greek mythology had the formidable faculty of growing two heads for every one that was cut off; and the dragons that we fight in history to-day often seem to mock and disconcert our victories with the same demonic contrariety. Is it not, for example, manifest that if goodness and moral sensitiveness develop so do the refinements of cruelty and wickedness? Does not man's very gain in power and knowledge constitute his deadliest temptation? Does not every fresh advance of Christ stimulate a new counteracting rejoinder of the devil? As at the first, the evil spirits recognise the menace to their sway—'Let us alone! What have we to do with Thee, Thou Jesus of Nazareth? Art Thou come to destroy us?'—and are quick to take action accordingly. Hence never here, it is held, within the historic process can Christ's empire be complete, never beneath the rising and setting sun will Jesus see of the travail of His soul, but only when the scroll of time has been wound up and history itself dissolved for ever by the mandate of the Lord.

Whatever else we may say about this view, at least it is realistic. At least it is immune from the temptation to by-pass Calvary, to prophesy smooth things about the natural perfectibility of man, and to romanticise a warfare in which there can be no discharge. At least it knows better than to ask us to believe the lie of a humanitarian inevitabilism, as though the momentum of the ages would by itself eliminate the blemishes by which life and history are now disfigured, and finally transform the desert of the world into the garden of the Lord. It is the strength of the apocalyptic outlook that it unmasks utopianism and gives the devil his due.

It has a further cogency, in that it supplies a salutary corrective to the type of religion which sets its heart on outward visible success. The clamour for impressive results stems sometimes at least from an anxiety complex in the Church: it bespeaks a tacit nervousness and fear that Christendom may be outmanoeuvred and left behind by the thrust and momentum of the emergent forces of modern secularism. Sometimes, too, no doubt, it derives from emulation of the methods of the world. Whatever its origin, it is a dangerous thing in a religion which is pledged to the way of the Cross. It is all too often a symptom that the Church has become infected by pagan standards. There is a way of seeking victory for the Christian cause which is a subtle apostasy from Christ. It is not the truest discipleship which needs the reassurance of demonstrable triumphs to buttress its faith and mitigate its feverishness. This may simply be a modern form of the ancient demand for a sign which Jesus emphatically rejected. To clutch greedily at external tokens of Christian prosperity and advance, to seek by means of material statistics to substantiate the view that the Kingdom has in it the potency of victory, to be depressed by what the world reckons failure and elated by what it would concede as success—this is a spirit for which our Lord's only comment may well be His grave word to Peter, 'Get thee behind Me, Satan: for thou savourest not the things that be of God, but the things that be of men.'

But there is another side to it. Over against the apocalyptic theology of mission, there is *another view that claims a hearing*. The late Principal D. S. Cairns once pointed out that nearly all the great missionary hymns of the Church envisage the spreading of the Gospel light throughout the world until the last shadows have been dispelled. Is this a hope we must renounce? Or can this be indeed the mainspring of our missionary motivation?

> Through the world far and wide
> > Let there be light.

> Nearer and nearer draws the time—the time that shall
> > surely be,
> When the earth shall be filled with the glory of God, as
> > the waters cover the sea.

> Thy Kingdom stands and grows for ever
> > Till all Thy creatures own Thy sway.

It is important to remark that this is not simply the old secular doctrine of progress being proclaimed with a Galilean accent. It is not idealism baptised into Christ. It stems from the Gospel itself. For from the hour when the new creation appeared in Jesus and the Kingdom of heaven entered history, God by His Spirit has been immanent in the Church which is Christ's Body; and there is no limit that can be assigned in history to the reach and penetration of the Cross and no end to the power of the Resurrection.

If this is accepted, it must be obvious at once that it has a vital bearing on missionary motivation. Doubtless it is right, as we have seen, to discountenance the clamour for visible results. But it is wrong to be suspicious of such results, when God in His loving kindness grants them. It is right to maintain the total irrelevance of worldly prowess and achievement to the religion of the Cross. But it is wrong to frown upon the expectation that great things will be seen happening when the Spirit of God goes mightily to work. It is no infidelity to the Cross to pray that the Lord may 'make bare His holy arm in the eyes of all the nations', nor is it any failure in humility to glory when He does it. It is no mark of defective spirituality to rejoice when revival breaks out and sweeps thousands into the Kingdom of God. It was when the seventy disciples returned from their first mission with the great news that even the devils were subject to them that 'Jesus rejoiced in spirit and said, I thank Thee, O Father, Lord of heaven and earth.'

It is one thing to be insistent on the irrelevance of outward success; it is quite another thing to allow that insistence to engender a depreciatory attitude towards movements of the Spirit in history. There is, in fact, an apocalyptic theology now current in certain quarters which, if its historical pessimism were carried to its logical issue, would discourage praying or toiling or evangelising for visible results of any kind at all, and would suggest that in proportion as missionary and evangelisistic results are tangible and impressive they must be meretricious and unreal. To this it ought to be replied that, if it is dangerous for the Church in the work of mission to corrupt the Gospel through being swayed by success, it is no less precarious for the Church to argue from the absence of success to the purity of the Gospel proclaimed. 'The same day,' records the Book of Acts, 'there were added unto them about three thousand souls.' 'And the Lord added to the Church daily such as should be saved.' To minimise such dramatic results of mission is a mark not of maturer spirituality but of plain ingratitude to God. There is a historical pessimism which betokens not faith but its reverse.

The fact is that it is entirely legitimate, while holding to the great Advent hope of the crowning victory hereafter, to pray and work for victories for Christ within history. Surely it is part of our missionary motivation to hope to see more and more areas of the corporate life of man being brought under the sway and dominance of Christ, and more and more lives 'turning from darkness to light and from the power of Satan unto God'. This, we are expressly told, was the motivation which the risen Christ imparted to Paul at Damascus. Is there any reason why the same hope should not remain to-day the valid inspiration and driving force of all our missionary endeavour?

There are, then, the two attitudes—they might be called the apocalyptic and the prophetic—which are not altogether easy to reconcile. Can the Bible resolve the difficulty for us? To this question we must now turn.

XIII

THE UNRESOLVED PARADOX

WHEN we turn to the Bible to resolve this matter for us, to decide between the two views of the goal of missions—the apocalyptic and the prophetic—the Bible would seem to speak now with one voice, now with the other.

Thus, on the one side, when the great missionary promise 'Lo, I am with you alway' was made radically eschatological in character by the addition of the phrase 'even unto the end of the age', might it not be held that such words implicitly *shatter history and look beyond for the glory of the Lord?* Nor can we miss the significance of the fact that, while our Lord declared that the message must be carried to all nations, He did not affirm that all nations would necessarily respond and pass out of death into life. That may be so, or it may not. What Jesus actually said was: 'This Gospel of the Kingdom shall be preached in all the world for a witness unto all nations: and then shall the end come.' It is further suggested in the parable of the wheat and the tares that the roots of good and evil are so inextricably intertwined that it will never in this world be possible to separate them out completely; never will you have a field, a culture, a society so fully Christian that the fruit of the Spirit can grow in peace, secure from the dark devices of the enemy; only at the harvest climax of God's final judgment can the tares be rooted out for ever. This does not look like the progressive penetration of history by the forces of light, and the gradual contraction down to vanishing-point of the empire of darkness. And what underlies that mysterious conception which flings a lurid light even across the pages of the New Testament, the colossal menace of the Antichrist—what but the sense that the demonic principalities and powers, so far from dwindling steadily into nothingness before the onward march of a militant evangelism, were indeed mustering their forces in reserve for the deadliest assault of all?

Still further, does not the New Testament conception of final judgment point in the same direction? That there are indeed interim judgments of God going on continually within history is quite clear. To the eye of faith, this is as clear amid the tensions and wars of the twentieth century as it was to the prophets of Israel who saw in Nebuchadnezzar and Cyrus the unconscious executors of the wrath of God. Such judgments, however, cannot be other than relative, since the historical forces which God uses to carry His judgments into effect are themselves involved in sin and far from perfect, and have therefore in their turn to be judged. But this does not mean that the concept of judgment remains tainted with relativism for ever. For the Cross on which Jesus died for love of men was itself the revelation of a holy God's implacable opposition to sin, the measure of the divine determination that evil shall finally be destroyed. The question therefore is this: is it conceivable that this irreversible dénouement can ever be reached amid the relativities of history? Must it not rather be that in the finalising of judgment by the act of God the whole pattern of history is destined to be shattered and dissolved?

Thus the apocalyptic view of victory beyond history is rooted indefeasibly in Scripture. But so also is the prophetic hope of *Christ's victory in the here and now*. Thus when Paul told the Corinthians that the God who at the first had said 'Let there be light' had now shone into men's hearts in Christ, he was asserting that the God of creation and the God of redemption were one. This is also the profound insight of the Johannine prologue: the Word becoming flesh and tabernacling amongst us for our redeeming is the same cosmic Word through whom in the beginning all things were made. Long before Paul and John, an old Hebrew poet had glimpsed dimly and from afar the same tremendous truth, when he linked together as the functions of Deity the counting of the number of the stars and the healing of the broken in heart. Now this has immense consequences for the prospects of the faith in history; for who, looking down the vistas of the future, can set limits to the recreating power of One who in the primordial miracle fashioned the cosmos out of nothing?

Paul himself went the length of affirming, in one of the most magnificently daring heights of speculation to which his thought ever rose, that it was not outside the bounds of possibility that even the material universe would ultimately share in the redemption provided for the sons of men, and be set free from frustration and decay: 'the creation itself shall be delivered from the bondage of corruption into the glorious liberty of the children of God.' Does this not suggest victory in history beyond our dreams? What gave the apostolic mission its glow and power and drive was the conviction that the God who had raised up Christ from the dead must be 'able to subdue all things unto Himself'; that it was the divine everlasting purpose to 'sum up all things in Christ'; that He who was the Alpha whence creation took its being must also be the Omega in whom it would find its rest; and that a day would come when 'in the name of Jesus every knee should bow and every tongue confess that Jesus Christ is Lord.'

Visible evidences and concrete phenomena were not lacking in that age to validate this hope. For everywhere the Gospel was producing indisputable results with which even the unbelieving world had to reckon. The Christian's citizenship in heaven might be concealed from the eyes of men; but unconcealed and open were his impact on society, his renovated ethic, his evangelising dynamic, his love and joy and peace. The world might know nothing of the Church's hidden mystical existence as the Body of Christ; but the world saw and commented with astonishment upon the destruction within the *koinonia* of racial barriers which hitherto had seemed impregnable. Graeco-Roman culture was increasingly feeling the impact—social, ethical and spiritual—of the new faith. If men could not tell whence the wind came nor whither it went, they did at least hear the sound of it, blowing where it listed.

Thus by many signs and tokens the apostles knew that their missionary labour was not in vain in the Lord. Indeed, it may well have appeared to them that Jesus' parable of the Kingdom was in process of being realised before their very eyes: 'It is like a grain of mustard seed, which when it is sown in the earth is less than all the seeds that be in the earth; but when it is sown, it groweth up and becometh greater than all herbs, and shooteth out great branches; so that the fowls of the air may lodge under the shadow of it.' Thus Paul bids the Colossians watch the Gospel penetrating into all the world, 'bearing fruit and increasing'. He instructs the Thessalonians to keep praying for the mission, 'that the word of the Lord may run and triumph'. Even the historic rejection of Israel is not final: once the Gentile mission has been fulfilled, the insensibility afflicting the chosen people shall have run its temporary course, and 'all Israel shall be saved'. It was no mood of extravagant phantasy that the men of the New Testament were indulging when they foresaw all the ends of the earth crowding in to Christ's allegiance, 'the kingdoms of this world becoming the Kingdom of our Lord and of His Christ'. For buttressing their hope like a firm, towering rock stood the prophetic word of the Johannine Christ: 'I, if I be lifted up from the earth, will draw all men unto Me.'

XIV

THE UNFINISHED TASK

IT would appear, then, from our study that the Bible does not immediately resolve the question as to the goal of missions. It gives a paradoxical answer. Sometimes the Scripture bids us lift up our eyes and look away beyond history; sometimes it spreads history itself before us and shows us Christ conquering and to conquer, God's will being done on earth as it is done in heaven. It may be that the conception of the Millennium in the Book of Revelation is designed to resolve the tension and transcend the paradox by maintaining the basic element of truth in both positions.

What, then, are we to say? *Is this question of the end of the missionary process perhaps one of the questions Christ declines to answer?* Is this one of the mysteries God refuses to unlock? It looks like this indeed. It may be this is the wisest conclusion we can reach.

If so, our missionary outlook must find room for both positions. *Victory beyond history*, yes—for always the Church on earth is under judgment, and never is its relation to the Kingdom of God one of simple identification. Always the conformation of Christian character to 'the measure of the stature of the fulness of Christ' is tainted with relativism, never finally free from sin, never perfect and complete. Always at every moment of his life man is a creature confronted with the necessity of decision, and therefore always needing to have an open road back to the Cross of Jesus for cleansing and renewal. Always the inexorable fact of mortality and corruption bestrides the portal to resurrection and eternal life: 'the last enemy that shall be destroyed is death.'

And may we not by analogy translate this into cosmic terms and hold that history too must die, that the historical process which is the corruptible body of mankind's spiritual pilgrimage must pass through that climax of destruction which is the only gateway to incorruption?

But indeed it is hardly likely that this aspect of the truth—victory beyond history—should be underemphasised in any modern theology of missions. The greater likelihood is a failure to stress the possibilities of *victory within history*. Surely it was not mere delusion nor theological ineptitude that kindled within the hearts of the great missionaries of the past the hope that Christ would use their toil and tears and blood for the advancement of His Kingdom upon earth. When we consider the amazing achievements of the faith of Christ through nineteen centuries, surely it is not baseless optimism to hope that concealed in the mists of the future other victories are waiting far surpassing in range and sweep and splendour anything that the past has known.

It is salutary in this connection to remember that we are still in a sense only at the very beginning of the Christian era. Measured by the standards of the vast expanses of time, the distance separating us from the mid-point of history, the Cross and the Resurrection, is only a hand's breadth. If the influence of Jesus has penetrated so deeply in the brief span of two thousand years, what might be its impact in two million?

It is indeed a daunting world that we look out upon, if we see only the human factors: there is no hope for history there, but ample grounds for fatalism and desperation. But the Christian insight recognises another factor in the scene, a factor of a new dimension, the dimension of the supernatural. The Word was made flesh. Ours is an essentially incarnational faith; and when

> He came down to earth from heaven
> Who is God and Lord of all,

it was a declaration that the world of supernature is most deeply concerned with the world of the material and the temporal. God does not stand apart from the historical process: He has involved Himself in it. This is the agelong travail of the soul of Christ. This is the love that will not let history go. This is the Spirit moving for ever upon the face of the waters, interpenetrating the chaos and the darkness with gleams of glory and energies of grace. This is the long-suffering of the Lord, which is salvation.

Hence an incarnational religion will always look out upon the world with a great and steadfast hope. It will find reassurance in the knowledge that the event of Bethlehem was sealed by the ascension and exaltation. For it was not to desert history that Christ returned to the Father, but to bind history to Himself for ever. Time enough, then, to despair of history when the Lord God omnipotent has abdicated the throne; time enough to yield to pessimism when Christ confesses that His passion was a blunder and the truth for which He died a lie. All Christians believe that God in Christ is working out His purpose in history through the Spirit; and human calculations cease to have any relevance to assess the operations of the Spirit. It is a verifiable phenomenon of Christian experience that an individual man, laid hold upon by the Spirit of God, can have his whole life lifted to a level of spiritual force and efficacy which previously would have seemed quite incredible; and if the Spirit of God can do such mighty works for and in and by one life surrendered to His sway, what a revolutionising of history might not result from a fully committed Church?

Moreover, there is a further basis of hope for those who envisage Christ triumphing in history. If we share the New Testament's insight that the victory of the Cross and the Resurrection happened 'once and for all', if this was indeed the finally decisive battle in the cosmic campaign between the Kingdom of God and the power of the demons, then it follows that the missionary assault upon the darkness of the world is facing a defeated enemy. The worst is past. Never again can the outcome of the conflict be in doubt. Never again will the cosmic issue tremble in the balance. Never again need the Messiah die or Calvary be refought. 'Jesus, being raised from the dead, dieth no more.' It happened once—never again—once and for all. 'It is finished,' was the cry on Golgotha.

This is not, of course, to close one's eyes to the appalling reality of evil in the present. It is not to minimise the toil and sweat of the conflict still remaining. But it *is* to declare that the watchword on the banner of the Church's mission, *Christus Victor*, represents not a pious hope but a historic, irrevocable fact. 'God was reconciling the world to Himself in Christ.' The divine accomplished deed stands towering over the struggle of the ages. The Bible knows nothing of an uneasy dualism, as though the Kingdom of God and the empire of evil were locked together in a perpetually indefinite and indecisive grapple. The initiative belongs to God. It is His world, not the devil's. Nothing can ultimately thwart His will. Even the most atrocious triumphs of iniquity are compelled in the end to subserve God's purposes, and not Satan's. And this being so, may we not joyfully and justly hope to see Christ triumphing gloriously *in history*, and His Gospel refashioning the world? Indomitably missionary will be the Church whose spirit has been kindled at the flame of this magnificent faith:

> The beam that shines from Zion hill
> Shall lighten every land;
> The King who reigns in Salem's towers
> Shall all the world command.

I have suggested that this question of the goal of missions which we have been considering—victory within history, or beyond—may be one of the questions Christ intentionally leaves unanswered. When His own disciples raised the question of the prospects of the Kingdom, 'It is not for you to know,' He answered: a trenchant commentary on the prophetic word—'My thoughts are not your thoughts, neither are your ways My ways, saith the Lord.' But what is dramatically significant is that, having said this, Jesus went on in the same breath to say—'You shall be witnesses unto Me in Jerusalem, Judaea, Samaria, and unto the uttermost part of the earth.'

The paradox of the Kingdom may be unresolved; but it is not in spite of that, it is precisely because of it, that the vocation to mission rings out trumpet-clear. It is not for you to see the end; it *is* for you to understand that the end cannot come until the Gospel has been preached to all the nations. It is not for you to read all history that may intervene between the decisive battle and Victory Day, between the Cross and the Parousia; it is for you to see that the intervening time is God's day of grace for men and nations, and that while it is day you must redeem the time and buy up the opportunity and carry everywhere the message of salvation before the hour of judgment strikes. It is not for you to search the times and seasons which the Father has kept in His own power; but it is for you, realising that man's disorder is alien to the Father's design and that it is not the Father's will that any life should perish, to rescue the perishing and smite the darkness and disorder with the dawn of truth and light.

Whatever the end, this is the present task. In the dispensation of God, this time in which we live is essentially the era of mission. Is it too much to hope that missionary obedience may not only make the crooked straight and the rough places plain but actually speed the Lord's return and hasten the final epiphany?